Brother or sister

Monica Hughes

Heinemann
LIBRARY

Little Nippers

www.heinemann.co.uk/library
Visit our website to find out more information about **Heinemann Library** books.

To order:
☎ Phone 44 (0) 1865 888066
▤ Send a fax to 44 (0) 1865 314091
▯ Visit the Heinemann Bookshop at www.heinemann.co.uk/library to browse our catalogue and order online.

First published in Great Britain by Heinemann Library, Halley Court, Jordan Hill, Oxford OX2 8EJ, part of Harcourt Education. Heinemann is a registered trademark of Harcourt Education Ltd.

Editorial: Sarah Eason and Georga Godwin
Design: Jo Hinton-Malivoire and Tokay, Bicester, UK (www.tokay.co.uk)
Picture Research: Rosie Garai and Sally Smith
Production: Séverine Ribierre and Alex Lazarus

Originated by Dot Gradations Ltd
Printed and bound in China by South China Printing Company

ISBN 0 431 18621 9 (hardback)
07 06 05 04 03
10 9 8 7 6 5 4 3 2 1

ISBN 0 431 18626 X (paperback)
08 07 06 05
10 9 8 7 6 5 4 3 2

British Library Cataloguing in Publication Data
Hughes, Monica
Brother or Sister – My First
306.8'75
A full catalogue record for this book is available from the British Library.

Acknowledgements
The Publishers would like to thank the following for permission to reproduce photographs:
Gareth Boden **pp. 4**, **5**, **6**, **7**, **8**, **9**, **10**, **12**, **13**, **14**, **15**, **16**, **17**, **19**, **20**, **21**, **22**, **23**; Masterfile/Albert Normandin **p. 11**; Masterfile/Brian Pieters **p. 18**.

Cover photograph is reproduced with permission of Gareth Boden.

The Publishers would like to thank Philip Emmett for his assistance in the preparation of this book. We would also like to thank Nicola, Steve and baby Louis.

Every effort has been made to contact copyright holders of any material reproduced in this book. Any omissions will be rectified in subsequent printings if notice is given to the Publishers.

Contents

I mum soo tongue g neu baby

A baby is on the way

I can't wait for the new baby to come.

Getting ready

Was I really this small once?

I help Mummy
pack her bag
for the hospital.

7

Gran comes to stay

Gran comes to look after me!

9

At the hospital

Hello, Mummy. I've missed you!

Hello, Baby!
I'm your
big brother.

11

Baby comes home

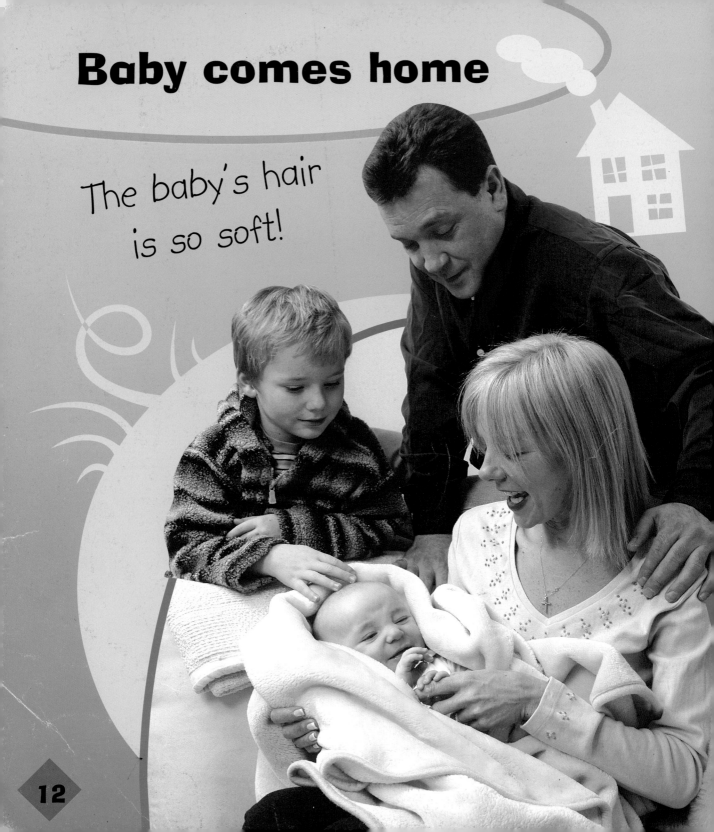

The baby's hair is so soft!

And she smells so nice.

Feeding

My baby sister spends a lot of time feeding.

Glug!

Glug!

Glug!

Sleeping

Zzzzzzzz! She even sleeps when we go for a walk!

What a noise!

Whaaaaaagh!

The baby is crying because she wants her milk.

18

I hope she stops crying and goes to sleep soon!

19

Helping with the baby

I'm good at helping to look after the baby.

He, he, he!

What would **you** do to help?

Babies grow and change

Index

The end

Notes for adults

This series supports the child's knowledge and understanding of their world, in particular their personal, social and emotional development. The following Early Learning Goals are relevant to the series:

• respond to significant experiences, showing a range of feelings where appropriate
• develop an awareness of their own needs, views and feelings and be sensitive to the needs and feelings of others
• develop a respect for their own cultures and beliefs and those of other people
• manage their own personal hygiene
• introduce language that enables them to talk about their experiences in greater depth and detail.

Each book explores a range of different experiences, many of which will be familiar to the child. It is important that the child has the opportunity to relate the content of the book to their own experiences. This will be helped by asking the child open-ended questions, using phrases like: How would you feel? What do you think? What would you do? Time can be made to give the child the chance to talk about their worries or anxieties related to the new experiences.

Talking about the new baby
The arrival of a new baby can seem quite daunting for the older child. They may need reassurance that they are still loved and 'special' even when their parents are busy with the baby. It may be possible to set aside a time each day when the older child can have the undivided attention of a parent. Together they could identify how the baby has changed – both positive and negative changes.

Further activities
Follow-up activities could involve comparing photographs of the older child when a baby with the new baby. The child could make a list of all the things a new baby can do (as well as crying!), and even make a name plate for the baby's room.